Stevie Wonder
EASY PIANO ANTHOLOGY

ISBN 978-0-634-00108-6

HAL•LEONARD®
CORPORATION
7777 W. BLUEMOUND RD. P.O. BOX 13819 MILWAUKEE, WI 53213

Visit Hal Leonard Online at
www.halleonard.com

I JUST CALLED TO SAY I LOVE YOU

Words and Music by
STEVIE WONDER

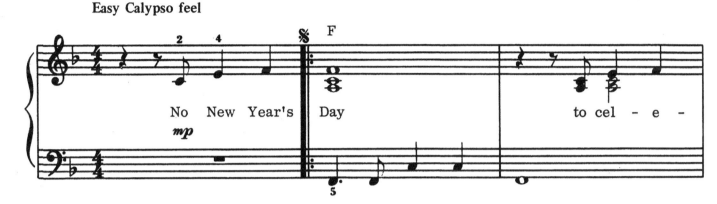

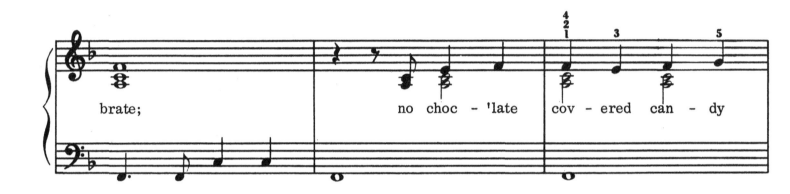

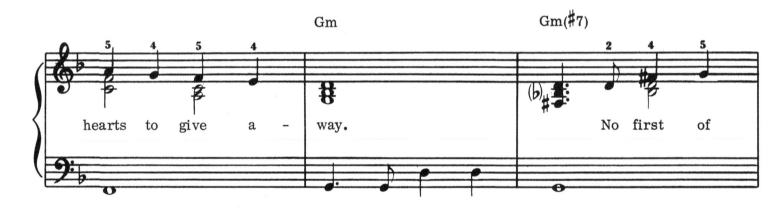

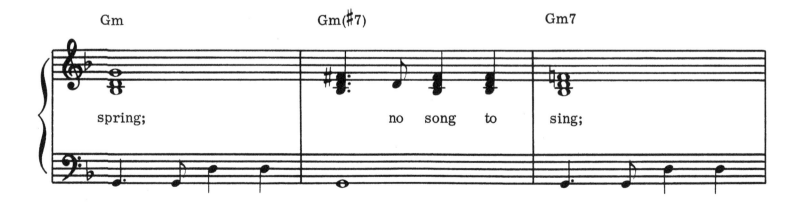

in fact, here's just an - oth - er or - din - ar - y

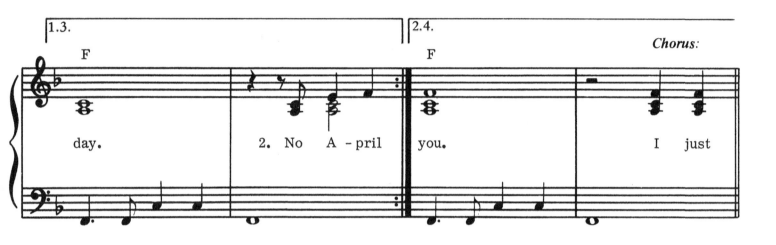

1.3. F
day.   2. No A - pril
2.4. F   Chorus:
you.   I just

Gm   C   F
called   to   say   I   love you.   I just

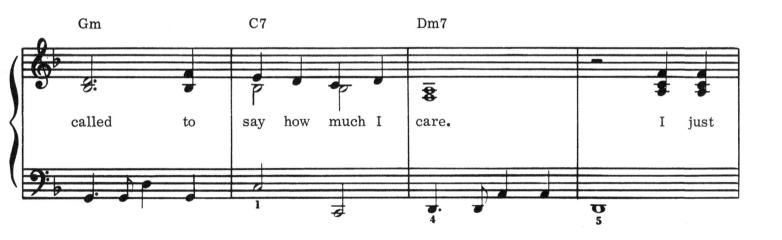

Gm   C7   Dm7
called   to   say how much I   care.   I just

4

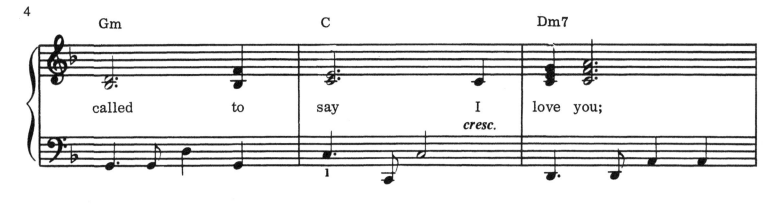

called to say I love you;
cresc.

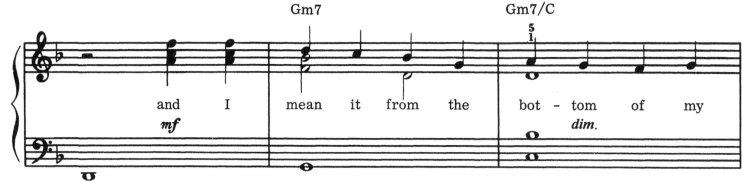

and I mean it from the bot - tom of my
mf *dim.*

heart. 3. No sum - mer's heart; of my
mp *cresc.*

heart; of my heart.

Verse 2: No April rain; no flowers bloom;
No wedding Saturday within the month of June.
But what it is, is something true,
Made up of these three words that I must say to you. *(To Chorus:)*

Verse 3:
No summer's high; no warm July;
No harvest moon to light one tender August night.
No autumn breeze; no falling leaves;
Not even time for birds to fly to southern skies.

Verse 4:
No Libra sun; no Halloween;
No giving thanks to all the Christmas joy you bring.
But what it is; though old, so new,
To fill your heart like no three words could ever do. *(To Chorus:)*

GOLDEN LADY

Words and Music by
STEVIE WONDER

1. Look-ing in your eyes,
2. Look-ing at your hands,

kind of heav - en eyes.
hands can un - der-stand.

Clos-ing both my eyes,
Wait-ing for the chance,

SIR DUKE

Words and Music by
STEVIE WONDER

Swing Tempo

Mu - sic is a world with - in it - self ____ with a
Mu - sic knows it is and al - ways will be one of

lan - guage we all un - der - stand, ____
the things that life just won't quit. ____

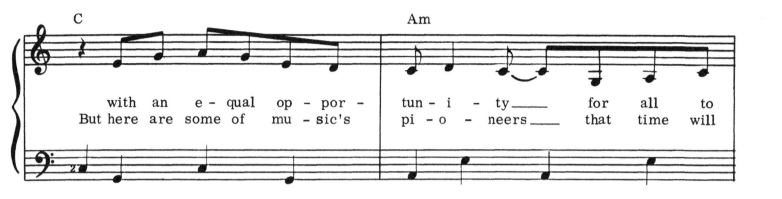

with an e - qual op - por -
But here are some of mu - sic's

tun - i - ty____ for all to
pi - o - neers____ that time will

sing,____ dance and clap their hands.____
not al - low us to for - get.____

But just be -
For there's

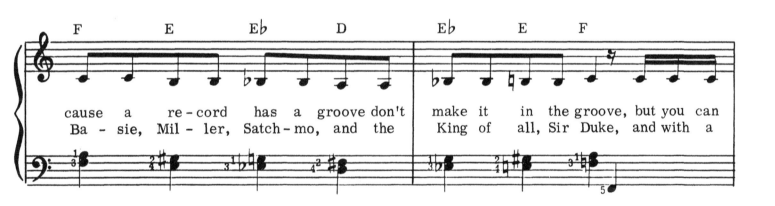

cause a re - cord has a groove don't
Ba - sie, Mil - ler, Satch - mo, and the

make it in the groove, but you can
King of all, Sir Duke, and with a

tell right a - way at let - ter "A" when the
voice like El - la's ring - in' out, there's no

peo - ple start to move.
way the band can lose.

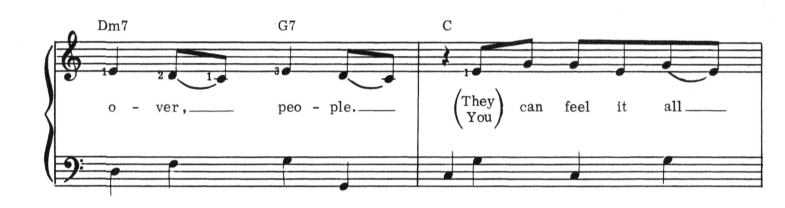

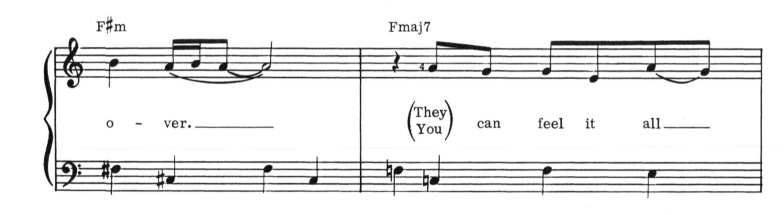

MY CHERIE AMOUR

Words and Music by STEVIE WONDER,
SYLVIA MOY and HENRY COSBY

Moderate

La la la la la la la la

la la la la My Che- rie A - mour,——
ca - fe —— or
some —— day —— or you'll

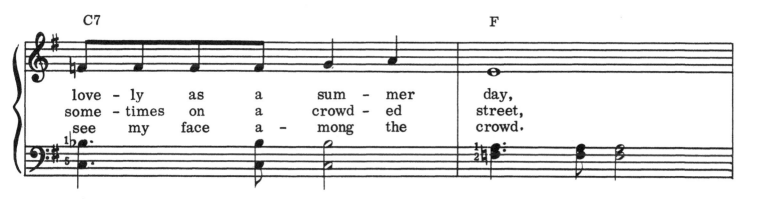

love - ly as a sum - mer day,
some - times on a crowd - ed street,
see my face a - mong the crowd.

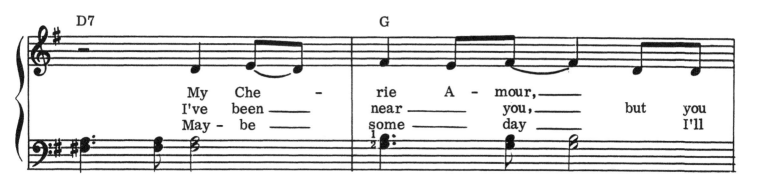

My Che- rie A - mour,——
I've been —— near —— you,—— but you
May - be —— some —— day —— I'll

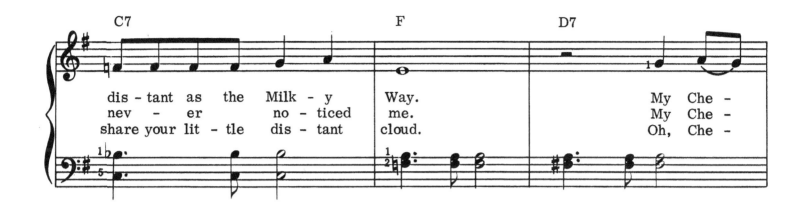

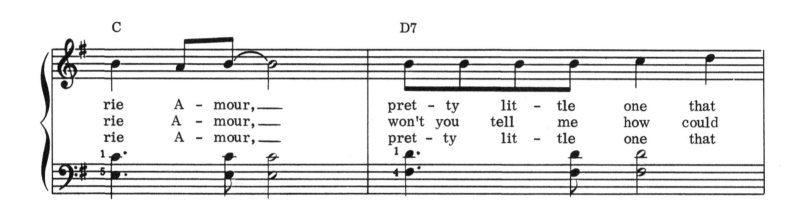

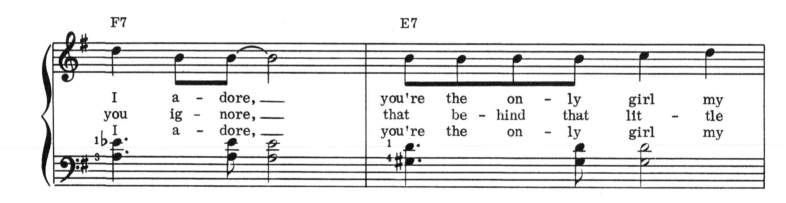

to Coda

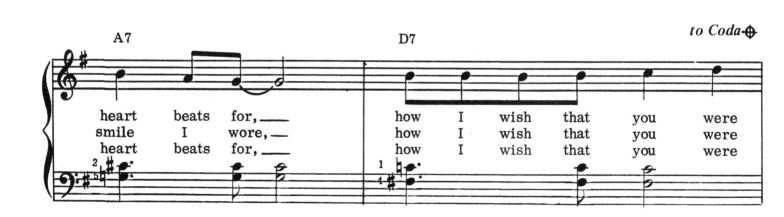

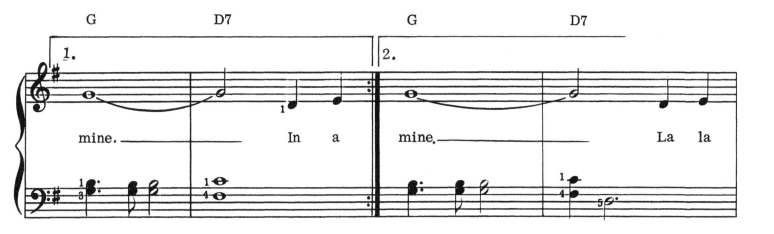

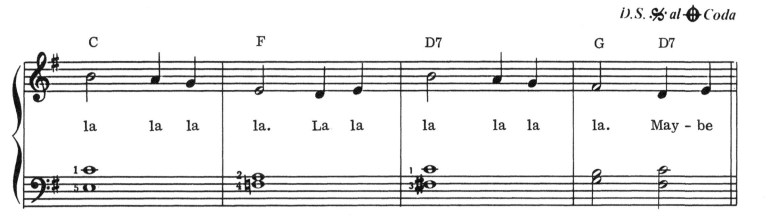

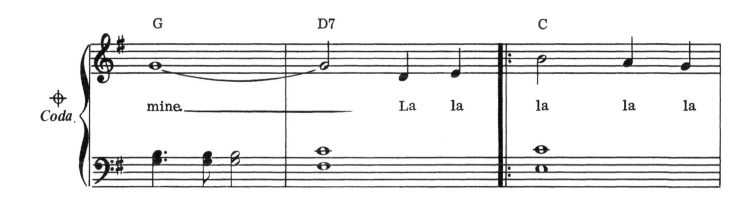

FOR ONCE IN MY LIFE

Words by RONALD MILLER
Music by ORLANDO MURDEN

SEND ONE YOUR LOVE

Words and Music by
STEVIE WONDER

18

UPTIGHT
(Everything's Alright)

Words and Music by STEVIE WONDER,
SYLVIA MOY and HENRY COSBY

Baby, ev-'ry-thing is all - right, up - tight,

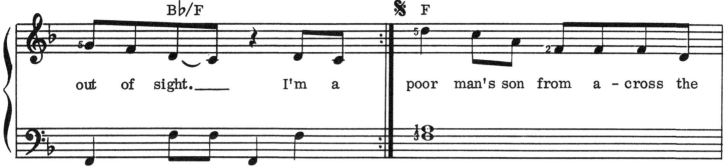

out of sight.___ I'm a poor man's son from a - cross the

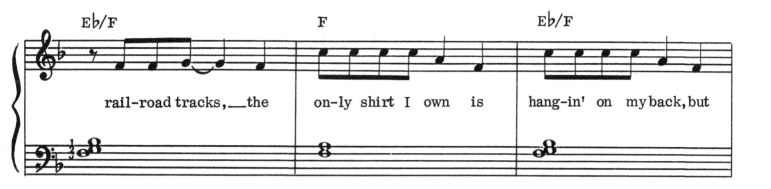

rail-road tracks,___ the on-ly shirt I own is hang-in' on my back, but

I'm ___ the en-vy of ev - 'ry sin - gle guy since

2. I'm a pearl of a girl, I guess that's what you might say,
   I guess her folks brought her up that way;
   The right side of the tracks, she was born and raised
   In a great big old house full of butlers and maids.

3. She says no one is better than I; I know I'm just an average guy,
   No football hero or smooth Don Juan; got empty pockets,
   You see, I'm a poor man's son.
   Can't give her the things that money can buy,
   But I'll never, never, never make my baby cry,
   And it's all right; what I can't do, out of sight, because my heart is true.

A PLACE IN THE SUN

Words and Music by RONALD MILLER
and BRYAN WELLS

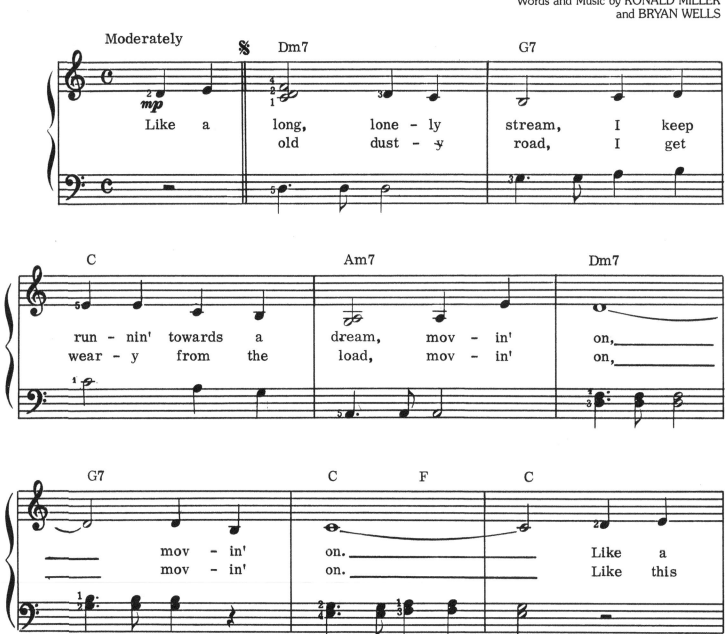

DO I DO

Words and Music by
STEVIE WONDER

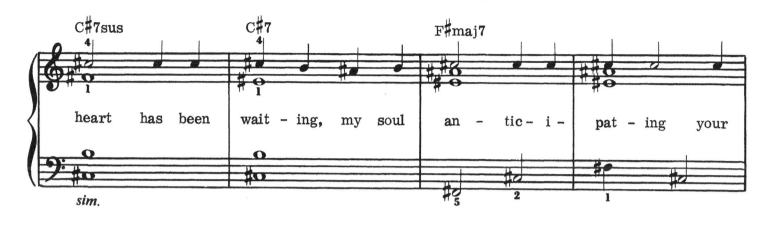

heart has been wait - ing, my soul an - tic - i - pat - ing your

sim.

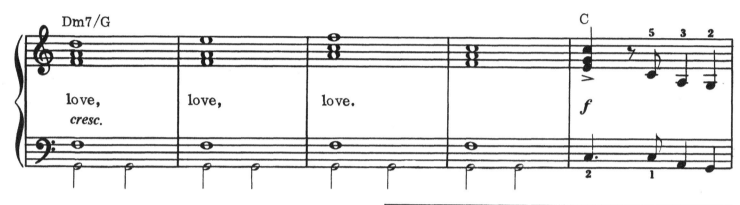

love, love, love.

cresc.

f

3. From___ the

Verse 2:
When I hear you on the phone,
Your sweet sexy voice turns my ear all the way on.
Just the mention of your name
Seems to drive my head insane.
Girl, do I do . . . etc.

Verse 3:
From the time that I awake
I'm imagining the good love that we'll make.
If to me your vibe can do all this
Just imagine how it's gonna feel when we hug and kiss.
Sugar, do I do . . . etc.

Verse 4:
I don't care how long it might take,
'Cause I know the woman for me – you I'll make.
'Cause I will not deny myself the chance
Of being part of what feels like the right romance.
Girl, do I do . . . etc.

SIGNED, SEALED, DELIVERED I'M YOURS

Words and Music by STEVIE WONDER, SYREETA WRIGHT,
LEE GARRETT and LULA MAE HARDAWAY

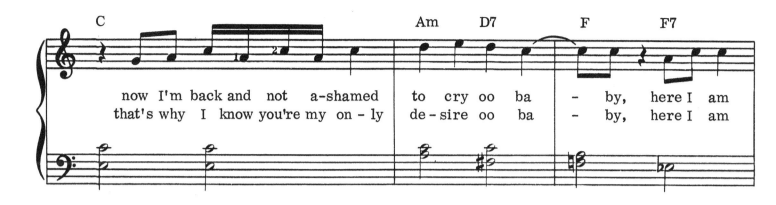

now I'm back and not a-shamed to cry oo ba - by, here I am
that's why I know you're my on - ly de - sire oo ba - by, here I am

signed, sealed, de-liv - ered, I'm yours.
signed, sealed, de-liv - ered, I'm yours.
Here I am,

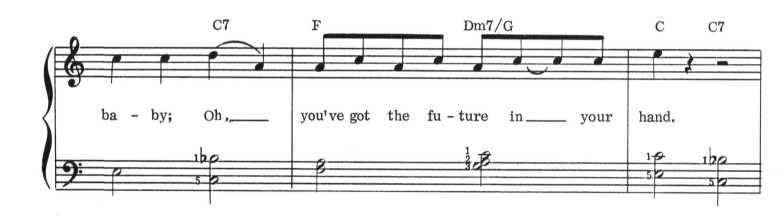

ba - by; Oh,___ you've got the fu - ture in___ your hand.

Here I am ba - by; Oh,___ you've got the fu - ture in___ your

YOU AND I

Words and Music by
STEVIE WONDER

Verse 2: Will it stay, the love you feel for me?
Will it say that you will be by my side to see me through;
Until my life is through?
(To Chorus:)

Verse 3: I am glad, at least in my life,
I found someone that may not be here forever to see me through;
But I found strength in you.

Verse 4: I only pray that I have shown you
A brighter day, because that's all that I am living for, you see;
Don't worry what happens to me.
(To Chorus:)

HIGHER GROUND

Words and Music by
STEVIE WONDER

Moderate Rock

Additional Lyrics: *(Repeat last 4 bars as written-sing additional lyrics below)*

Don't you let nobody bring you down. They'll sho' nuff try.
God is gonna show you Higher Ground. He's the only friend you have around.

DON'T YOU WORRY 'BOUT A THING

Words and Music by
STEVIE WONDER

Moderate Latin Rhythm

3. Ba - bum - ba - bum - ba - bum, ba - bum.
   Bum, bum, bum, bum, bum, bum, bum.

4. Ev'rybody needs a change, a chance to check out the new.
   But you're the only one to see, the changes you take yourself through.
   Don't you worry 'bout a thing. Don't you worry 'bout a thing, pretty mama,
   'Cause I'll be standin' in the wings when you check it out.

THAT GIRL

Words and Music by
STEVIE WONDER

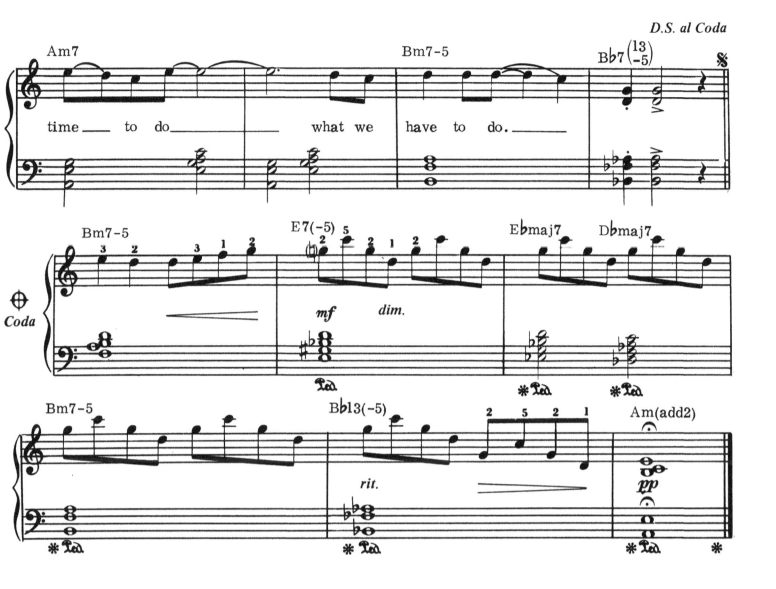

Verse 2:

That girl thinks that she's so bad, she'll change my tears to joy from sad.
She says she keeps the upper hand, 'cause she can please her man.
She doesn't use her love to make him weak, she uses love to keep him strong;
And inside me there's no room for doubt that it won't be too long
Before I tell her that I ...*(To Chorus:)*

Verse 3:

That girl knows every single man would ask for her hand;
But she says her love is much too deep for them to understand.
She says her love has been crying out, but her lover hasn't heard;
But what she doesn't realize, is that I've listened to every word.
That's why I know I'll tell her that I ... *(To Chorus:)*

SUPERSTITION

Words and Music by
STEVIE WONDER

46

FINGERTIPS
(Part 2)

Words and Music by CLARENCE O. PAUL
and HENRY COSBY

loud - er,   clap your hands ____   just   a lit - tle bit loud -   er.

Dm   G   Dm   G   Dm

(4 times)

Dm   G   Dm   G   Dm

(4 times)   I   know that I nev-er got to   hey yeah. Ev-'ry-

BOOGIE ON REGGAE WOMAN

Words and Music by
STEVIE WONDER

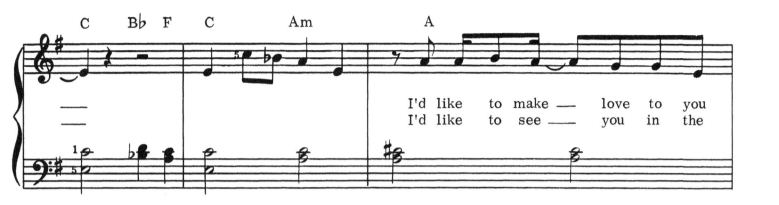

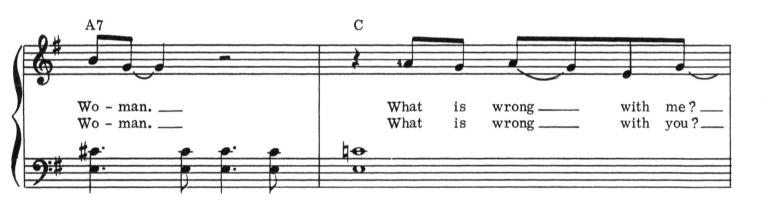

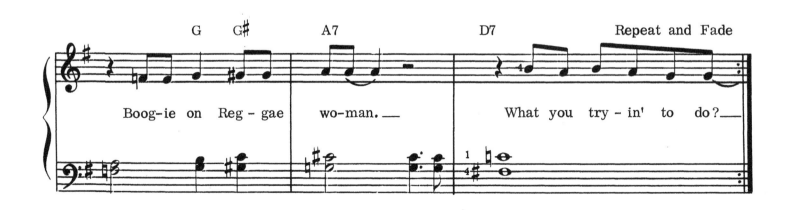

I BELIEVE
(When I Fall in Love It Will Be Forever)

Words and Music by STEVIE WONDER
and YVONNE WRIGHT

Slowly

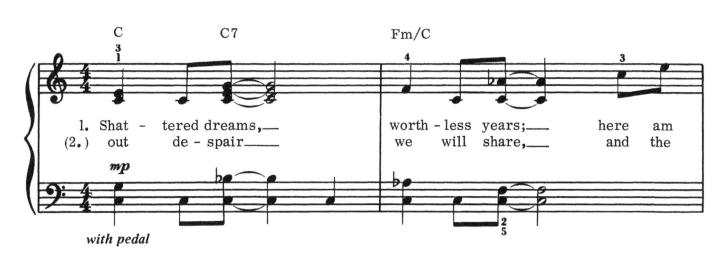

1. Shat - tered dreams,___ worth - less years;___ here am
(2.) out de - spair___ we will share,___ and the

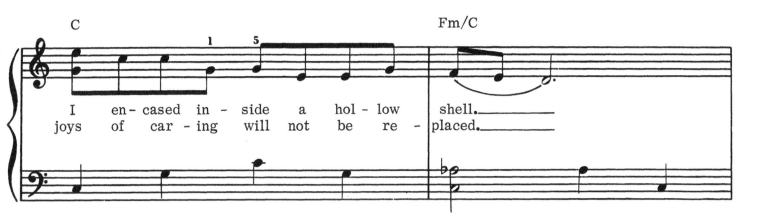

I en - cased in - side a hol - low shell.___
joys of car - ing will not be re - placed.___

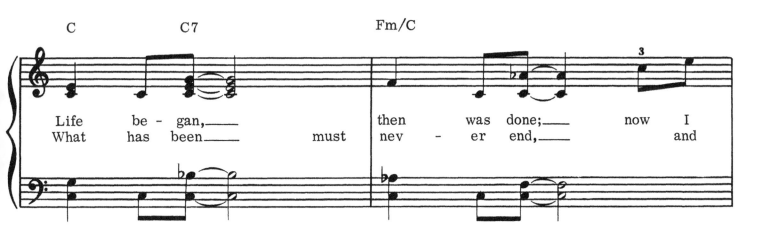

Life be - gan,___ then was done;___ now I
What has been___ must nev - er end,___ and

54

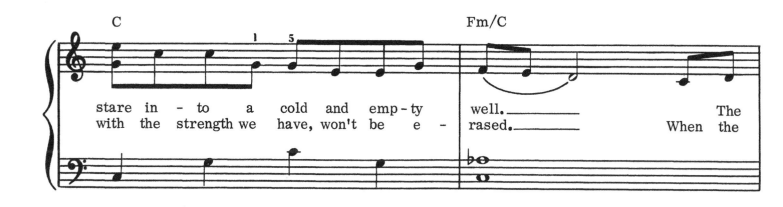

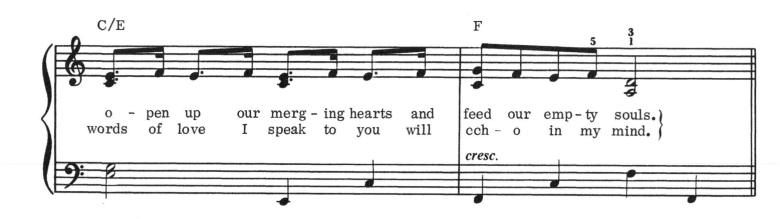

Chorus:

YESTER-ME, YESTER-YOU,
YESTERDAY

Words by RON MILLER
Music by BRYAN WELLS

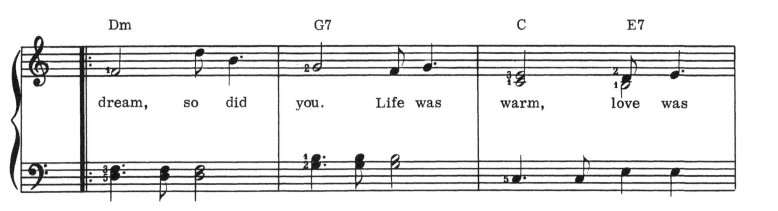

Dm — dream, so did you. G7 — Life was C — warm, love was E7

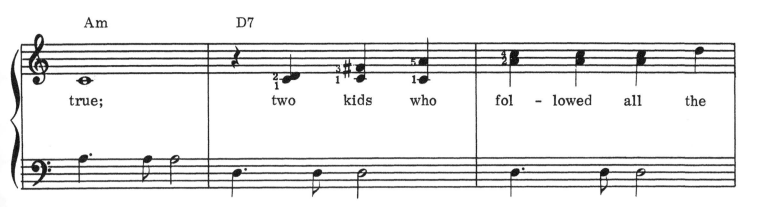

Am — true; D7 — two kids who fol - lowed all the

1st time D S. to 2nd ending
2nd time D. S. to fine

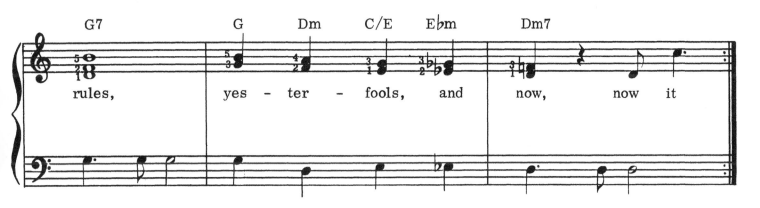

G7 — rules, G — yes - ter - Dm C/E fools, and E♭m Dm7 — now, now it

2. Where did it go, that yester-glow
    When we could feel the wheel of life turn our way?
    Yester-me, yester-you, yester-day,
    When I recall what we had,
    I feel lost, I feel sad
    With nothing but the mem'ry of yester-love
    And now, now it (coda)

SHOO BE DOO BE DOO DA DAY

Words and Music by STEVIE WONDER,
SYLVIA MOY and HENRY COSBY

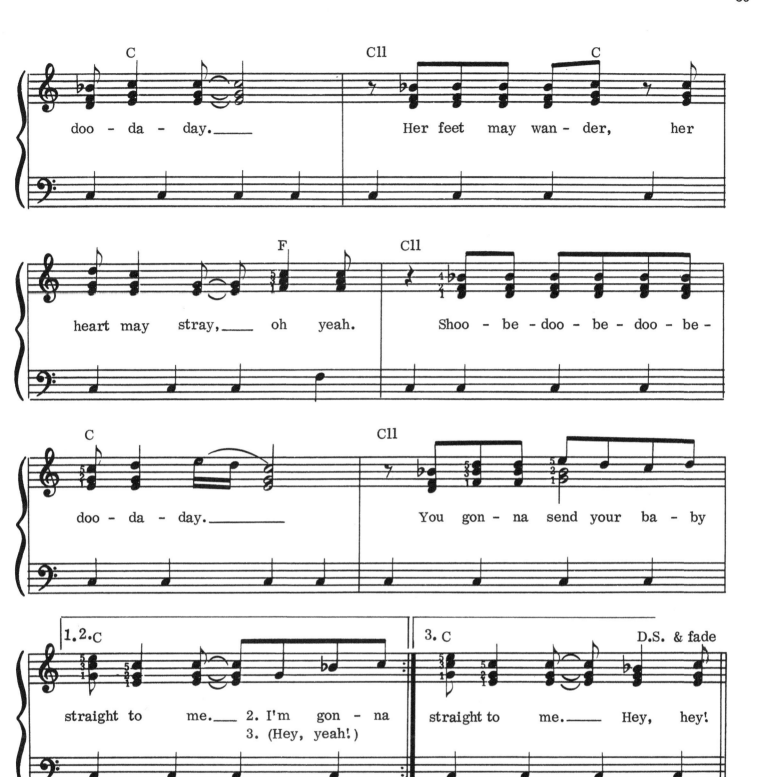

2. (I'm gonna) give her all the lovin' within my heart, oh yeah,
   I'm gonna patch up every single little dream you tore apart.
   Understand me?
   And when she tells you she's cried her last tear,
   Heaven knows, I'm gonna be somewhere near, oh yeah. (Chorus)

3. (Hey, yeah), heartaches are callin', tears are fallin' because of you, hey yeah.
   And when you're gone, she'll know I'm the one to go to her rescue.
   Baby, you didn't know that thing.
   You're gonna leave her once too many times,
   And when you come back that girl's gonna be mine, all mine, hey!

LIVING FOR THE CITY

Words and Music by
STEVIE WONDER

Moderate

2. His sister's black, but she is sho' nuff pretty.
   Her skirt is short, but Lord her legs are sturdy.
   To walk to school, she's got to get up early.
   Her clothes are old, but never are they dirty.

   Her brother's smart, he's got more sense than many.
   His patience's long, but soon he won't have any.
   To find a job is like a haystack needle,
   'Cause where he lives they don't use colored people.
   Living just enough - Just enough for the city.

3. His hair is long, his feet are hard and gritty.
   He spends his life walkin' the streets of New York City.
   He's almost dead, from breathing in air pollution.
   He tried to vote, but to him there's no solution.

   I hope you hear, inside my voice of sorrow,
   And that it motivates you to make a better tomorrow.
   This place is cruel, no where could be much colder.
   If we don't change, the world will soon be over.
   Living just enough - Just enough for the city.

I WAS MADE TO LOVE HER

Words and Music by STEVIE WONDER, LULA MAE HARDAWAY,
SYLVIA MOY and HENRY COSBY

Moderately Slow

I WISH

Words and Music by
STEVIE WONDER

Brightly (not too fast)

Look - ing back on when I was a lit - tle nap - py - head - ed boy, ___ then my on - ly wor - ry was for Christ - mas what would be my toy. ___ Ev - en though we some - times

70

so. Do do do do do do do do do do do do,

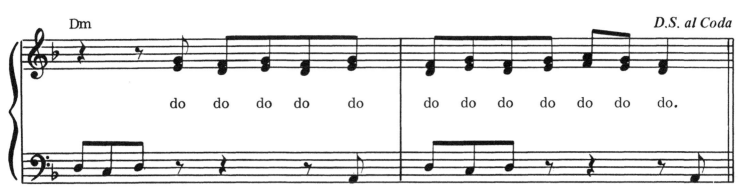

do do do do do do do do do do do do.

D.S. al Coda

Repeat and Fade

Coda

(so.)

Brother says he's tellin'
'Bout you playin' doctor with that girl
Just don't tell, I'll give you
Anything you want in this whole wide world.
Mama gives you money for Sunday school
You trade yours for candy after church is through.

Smokin' cigarettes and writing something nasty on the wall (you nasty boy).
Teacher sends you to the principal's office down the hall.
You grow up and learn that kinda thing ain't right
But while you were doin' it - it sure felt outta sight.

I wish those days could come back once more.
Why did those days ev--er have to go?
I wish those days could come back once more.
Why did those days ev--er have to go?
'Cause I loved them so.

RIBBON IN THE SKY

Words and Music by
STEVIE WONDER

Verse 2:
If allowed, may I touch your hand,
And if pleased, may I once again,
So that you too will understand
There's a ribbon in the sky for our love?

Verse 3:
This is not a coincidence,
And far more than a lucky chance,
But what is that is always meant
Is our ribbon in the sky for our love.

Verse 4:
We can't lose with God on our side.
We'll find strength in each tear we cry.
From now on it will be you and I
And our ribbon in the sky, ribbon in the sky,
A ribbon in the sky for our love.

YOU ARE THE SUNSHINE OF MY LIFE

Words and Music by
STEVIE WONDER

Moderately, with feeling

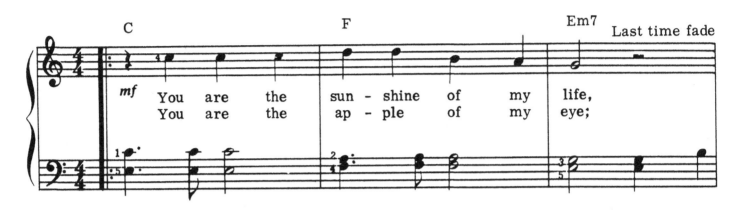

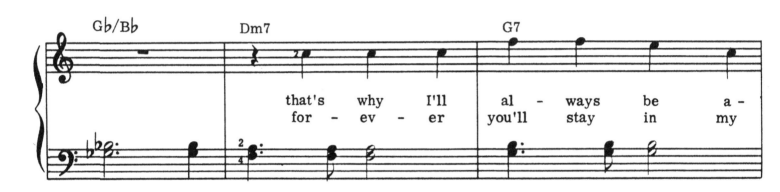

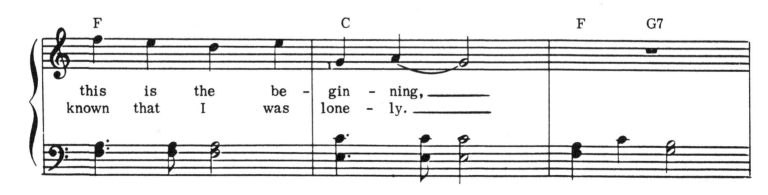

ISN'T SHE LOVELY

Words and Music by
STEVIE WONDER

ALL IN LOVE IS FAIR

Words and Music by
STEVIE WONDER

Verse 2:
All of fate's a chance;
It's either good or bad.
I tossed my coin to say,
In love with me you'd stay,
But all in war is cold.
You either win or lose;
When all is put away,
The losing side I'll play,
But all is fair in love,
I should have never left your side.
A writer takes his pen
To write the words again,
That all in love is fair.
(To 2nd ending)